Editor
Mandy Cleeve

Assistant Editor
Virginie Verhague

Designer
Andy Archer

Publishing Director
Jim Miles

Authors
Angela Royston, Linda Sonntag,
Jill Thomas

Proofreaders
Charlotte Evans, Penny Williams

Picture Researchers
Su Alexander, Elaine Willis

Artwork Archivist
Wendy Allison

Assistant Artwork Archivist
Steve Robinson

KINGFISHER
An imprint of Larousse plc
Elsley House,
24-30 Great Titchfield Street
London
W1P 7AD

First published by Larousse plc 1995

(hb) 10 9 8 7 6 5 4 3 2 1
(pb) 10 9 8 7 6 5 4 3 2 1

A CIP catalogue record for this book is available
from the British Library

ISBN 1 85697 477 4 (hb)
ISBN 1 85697 369 7 (pb)

Printed in Scotland

CONTENTS

6

MENACE ON THE MOON

The Moon is dry and lifeless. It has no air or water, so there is no wind, no weather and no sound. It is blazing hot during the day, but freezing cold at night. The Moon orbits the Earth and together they orbit the massive Sun. The Moon is about 50 times smaller than Earth and its pull of gravity is six times weaker. On his lunar adventure, Dennis can jump six times as high as he can on Earth! With no light of its own, the Moon only seems bright in the sky because it reflects the light of the Sun.

In the museum —

SPACE

Let's hide from the Mayor, Gnasher!

1 Some scientists believe that the Moon formed when a giant meteoroid the size of Mars crashed into the young, red-hot Earth.

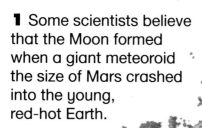

2 The explosion sent a colossal cloud of hot dust and rocks into orbit around the Earth. The cloud fused to form the Moon.

▷The side of the Moon we can see has huge plains of lava, called seas. But one half of the Moon is always hidden from us. No one had ever seen the far side until a spacecraft photographed it in 1959.

LUNAR FACTS

The Moon is almost as wide as Australia. It is 3,476 km across.

Everything — even meteoroid explosions — occur in total silence.

If Earth was the size of a football, the Moon would be as big as an apple lying just 7 m away.

Laser beams are now able to measure the distance to the Moon with an accuracy of about 10 cm!

Despite its violent history, the Moon's surface has remained virtually unchanged for billions of years — since life on Earth first began.

Earth weighs a massive 81 times as much as the Moon.

The first people to set foot on the Moon were the astronauts Neil Armstrong and Edwin Aldrin. They landed in *Apollo 11* on July 20, 1969.

In here till the heat dies down!

Wouldn't it be great if this space ship works!

SPACE SHUTTLE

It does! Moon here we come!

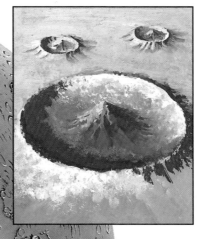

△ When the Moon was new, it was a smouldering globe of rock. As the surface cooled, it formed a crust. Chunks of iron and metal called meteoroids crashed into the surface and exploded like bombs. There were so many explosions that some craters overlap. The largest is the Imbrium Basin, a staggering 1,100 km wide!

Today Dennis the Menace is in orbit around the Moon.

Gasp! No wonder it's quiet around here!

△ There is no wind on the Moon to wipe away the astronauts' footprints. The tracks in the Moondust will last forever — unless someone disturbs them.

DENNIS IN ORBIT

The Earth and Moon are part of the Solar System — the Sun and the family of planets, asteroids and comets that orbit around it. The huge size and gravity of the Sun keeps the Solar System in place and controls the spin of the planets. The Sun also provides all our light and heat. It is already 4,600 million years old, but luckily it has enough fuel to shine for another 5,000 million years. Earth is the only planet to support life. Although astronomers think the Universe must hold other planets like ours, none have been found yet — so don't stray too far Dennis!

Wonder if we could speak to an alien!

COMMUNICATIONS SCREEN

ON

Mercury

Jupiter

Venus

Earth

Mars

WHIRLING WORLDS

A day on Mercury is longer than its year! Mercury takes longer to spin on its axis than it does to orbit the Sun.

Venus is so blisteringly hot that it soon destroys any space probes landing on it.

Billions of years ago, Mars was wet and damp. Its iron-rich surface rusted, turning Mars into a red planet.

Jupiter is so big it could fit all the other planets inside it.

Saturn has at least 18 moons, more than any other planet. Most of them are just enormous, rocky snowballs.

Uranus is tipped over so it rolls on its side. It also spins backwards.

Bright blue Neptune may look calm, but its fierce winds can rage at 2,200 km/h.

Pluto was only discovered in 1930. No probe has ever visited this frozen world.

△ Mercury, Venus, Earth and Mars are the four planets closest to the Sun. They consist mainly of rock and metal. Only Earth has water on its surface. Mars has air, but its atmosphere is mainly carbon dioxide — we could not breathe it.

▷ Jupiter, Saturn, Uranus and Neptune are called Gas Giants. There is no solid surface for astronauts (or Dennis) to land on. Tiny Pluto has an odd, looping orbit. Usually it is the furthest planet from the Sun, but once every 248 years Pluto swings in closer than Neptune.

Uranus

Probes and telescopes help us learn more about the Solar System and beyond. The Hubble Space Telescope can see images much more clearly than ground-based observatories. Orbiting at 580 km up, Hubble avoids Earth's atmosphere which distorts and blurs the light from the stars. It is able to see past our Solar System to millions of distant galaxies.

Saturn

Neptune

Pluto

◁ What lies beyond Pluto? Some star-gazers believe there might be a tenth planet. But this mysterious 'Planet X' may not be a planet at all — it could be a huge comet or even an enormous black hole.

Tune in next week for part two!

Oops! Looks like we just picked up a satellite channel!

11

MIGHTY MILKY WAY

Our Sun is just one star among billions in our galaxy, the Milky Way. You can see the Milky Way from Earth. On a clear, moonless night it looks like a broad band of misty light, but it is in fact a huge collection of stars, gas and dust held together by gravity. The Milky Way is spinning. It is so enormous, it takes the Sun 225 million years just to go round once! It is vaster than anything Dennis could imagine, but it is only a tiny part of the whole Universe. The Milky Way is shaped like a spiral. Around the centre is a nucleus of red giants, the remains of ancient suns.

You drive, Gnasher. I want to look at the Milky Way!

GALACTIC FACTS

There are over 100 billion stars in the Milky Way. Don't try to count them — it would take 3,000 mind-boggling years! And there are at least a staggering 100 billion other galaxies in space.

Our galaxy is so massive that a light beam travelling 300,000 km/h takes 100,000 years to cross from one side to the other.

Compared to other galaxies, the Milky Way is still young even though it is 14 billion years old!

The Milky Way is hurtling through space at over 2,000,000 km/h — fast enough to get from London to New York in 10 seconds.

Some astronomers believe a black hole lies at the centre of the Milky Way.

The closest star to our Sun is Proxima Centauri. Our nearest neighbour in the Milky Way, it lies 4.2 light years away. It is so distant even the strongest telescopes cannot see whether it has planets orbiting around it.

The Milky Way is creating new stars all the time. One is produced about every 18 days!

12

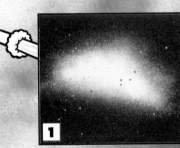

From the side, the Milky Way looks like a swollen disc. The arrow shows the position of our Sun.

Our galaxy is so massive that light from the centre takes about 30,000 years to reach us on Earth!

◁This is how we see the Milky Way from Earth. The dark patches in the sky are huge clouds of gas which hang between the stars. These dusty shadows totally obscure the centre of our galaxy, which blazes with the light of old stars.

◁Galaxies come in all kinds of shapes!
1 Irregular (no shape)
2 Elliptical (egg-shaped)
3 Spiral

BAFFLING BLACK HOLES

Black holes are not holes at all. They are round, solid objects formed by the death of a giant star. When a star has burnt all of its fuel, it dies. If the star is vast, it may leave behind a super-dense core of material just a few kilometres wide, called a neutron star. Its gravity is so strong, it pulls other material into itself. Everything is sucked in — from gas to solid objects like Dennis' spaceship. Even light can't escape! As more falls in the black hole gets heavier, pushing its horizon wider and wider.

A black hole — turn for home, Gnasher!

SWERVE!

DARK FACTS

Some astronomers believe that the more a black hole 'eats' the bigger it gets. If so, some greedy black hole giants may be gobbling the equivalent of 3 Earths every single second.

Tiny neutron stars were once giant stars 3 or 4 times bigger than our Sun. There are probably millions of neutron star black holes in the Milky Way alone.

A black hole turns space inside-out. From outside it looks like a round black object, only a few kilometres across. But from the inside it seems as big as the Universe — you could see nothing beyond it.

Supernovas are very rare — even if you observed 100 billion stars, it would be 25 years before an explosion took place.

▷As no light can get out of a black hole, how can you see it? It's impossible, but you can tell that it is there by watching matter being sucked into it. As it gets dragged in the matter heats up. It then radiates some energy away as it spirals into oblivion. So the dark centre of a black hole has a halo of light.

◁If Earth was compressed to the density of a neutron star, it would only be as wide as a sports field. A marble-sized ball of this matter would weigh more than a million loaded juggernauts!

14

A black hole acts like a vast one-way funnel in space. Its overwhelming gravitational pull swallows anything that passes too close. Gas, dust and light disappear into it like water down a plug hole.

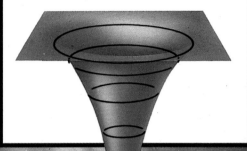

A supernova is the death of a huge star, bigger than our Sun. When a star collapses it triggers a colossal explosion. In seconds, temperatures reach 5,000 million °C! If the star is very heavy it caves in so much that it becomes a black hole.

Wonder what we'd look like if we'd fallen into the black hole?

PUZZLING PLATES

The Earth is an immense, rocky ball. It is so wide that it would take Minnie more than a year to trudge round it — even if she walked night and day! Earth's surface is broken into plates which fit together like pieces in a huge jigsaw puzzle. These slabs float on a layer of molten rock, carrying the continents and ocean floor with them. The movements are so tiny that we do not usually notice them. But sometimes they can be very strong. When two plates bang into each other, they can push up mountains, create volcanoes or cause earthquakes.

This is the section for me!

PLANET EARTH

▷ Earth is covered by a fragile crust. This layer is wafer-thin. If Earth shrank to the size of a metre-wide ball, it would only be 1.5 mm deep!

Crust

Mantle

Core

▽ As Minnie journeys deeper down, it gets much warmer. Below the thin surface is the mantle, a layer of molten rock which flows in thick, slow currents. In the middle lies the solid metal core, the hottest part of all. There the temperature could be a searing 7,000 °C — as sizzling as the surface of the Sun!

SHUDDERING SHOCKS

There are half a million earthquakes a year, but only 1 in 500 causes damage.

Can animals sense earth tremors? In 1975 the Chinese city of Haicheng was evacuated 2 hours before a quake, because people noticed their pets behaving oddly.

The longest earthquake ever recorded lasted for 38 days!

The continental plate of North America moves about 3 cm away from Europe every year.

The strongest earthquake ever recorded took place on May 22, 1960 at Lebu on the west coast of Chile in South America.

Geothermal power stations harness the heat trapped inside the Earth to create electricity.

> One way to measure earthquakes is by using the Richter scale. This grades earthquake energy. Each time a tremor moves a number up the scale, 32 times as much energy is being released!

1.2 Barely noticeable

5 Some damage

7 Like a nuclear bomb

8 Total devastation

△ When one plate slides against another, shock waves are sent out in all directions. Some collisions take place over 720 km below the surface.

The Trans-America Pyramid in San Francisco, USA has been specially designed so that it will resist collapse even during a violent earthquake. Earthquake-proof buildings are very flexible. This allows them to bend and sway without shattering. But their foundations are built on a solid platform, embedded deep in the rock.

MOLTEN MINX

When a volcano explodes it throws ash, rocks and dust high into the sky. Minnie will gasp for air when she smells the suffocating gases! Molten rock called lava spurts out and flows down the mountainside like a river of red-hot mud. Some volcanoes can 'sleep' for many years or even 'die', but more than 1,300 are active. Geysers are found in volcanic areas as well. Instead of showering lava, geysers throw out jets of steam and hot water. Heat below the Earth's surface also erupts in bubbling hot springs and boiling mud pools.

You're wrong if you think this planet's boring . . .

. . . when you can bore down into a volcano!

Extinct volcanoes

Lava flow

EXPLODING FACTS

In 1963 the island of Surtsey suddenly appeared in the sea off Iceland. It was made by an undersea volcano.

Old Faithful, a geyser in Yellowstone National Park in the United States, shoots a jet of water and steam into the air about once every 70 minutes. It has been doing this for over 80 years!

When Krakatoa in Indonesia exploded in 1883 the rumble could be heard in Australia, 5,000 km away. The cloud of ash was so thick, the island was in darkness for 3 days.

Imagine playing on a beach of coal dust! That's what the black, lava sand on the island of Vulcano near Italy looks like.

▷ Don't fall down a volcano! At the bottom of the long 'chimney' is a huge chamber of hot, molten rock called magma. As the pressure builds up, magma bursts out through a crack in the ground and spews out as burning lava. This flowing stream is scalding hot. Its temperature can be more than 1,200 °C — that's 12 times hotter than boiling water!

Geysers are found where hot rocks lie near to the Earth's surface. Just like a pressure cooker, underground pockets of water are heated up until they pass boiling point. Then super-heated steam and water are thrown out of the ground in explosive jets. In New Zealand, the highest geyser ever seen produced fountains that reached over 460 m high.

Geyser

Hot springs

Layers of ash and lava

Central vent

Magma chamber

△ In AD 79 the volcano of Vesuvius in Italy erupted, covering the entire city of Pompeii with cinders and rocks. People were buried alive, leaving the shape of their bodies preserved in the ash. This baker was found next to a loaf of bread he had just made.

AWESOME OCEANS

The Earth looks blue from space. That's because nearly three-quarters of it is covered by water — seas, oceans, rivers and lakes. Water is also locked up as ice at the poles and as vapour in the atmosphere. But the great oceans account for 97 per cent of all the water on Earth. Their salty water comes from rocks worn down by wind and rain, and washed into the sea by rivers. Let's hope Minnie is a good swimmer because the oceans are never still — sometimes they rage violently! Currents flow through the sea like rivers and winds send huge waves rolling across its surface.

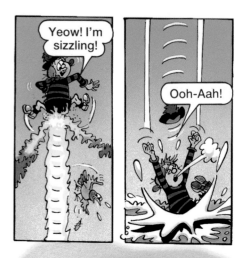

> Yeow! I'm sizzling!

> Ooh-Aah!

The Dead Sea in Asia is actually a lake, the lowest land area on Earth. It is also the saltiest body of water in the world — an astonishing nine times more salty than ordinary seawater. The water is so dense even non-swimmers find it impossible to sink!

▽ The Mariana Trench in the Pacific is the deepest point in the oceans. If you stood Mount Everest at the bottom its tip would still be 2,000 m below the surface!

▽ The ocean floor has a landscape of mountains and deep, deep trenches. If Minnie splashed down on a sunny tropical island, it could actually be the tip of an undersea volcano.

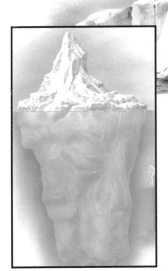

△Gigantic blocks of ice float in the Arctic and Antarctic oceans. They tower over ships, but nine-tenths of the ice is hidden below the waves. The largest ever known was as big as the country of Belgium!

▽Tsunamis are huge tidal waves. They travel as fast as jet airliners, but the earth tremors that cause them move 50 times faster.

SPLASHING FACTS

Tsunamis can loom up to 85 m high — at least as tall as a colossal thirty-storey skyscraper!

If all the ice at the North and South poles melted, London, New York and thousands of other cities would be drowned in seawater.

There is 4 g of gold in every million tonnes of seawater.

The Pacific Ocean is the world's largest ocean. It is also bigger than all the continents put together.

The oceans filled up 4,000 million years ago when it rained non-stop for over 60,000 years!

Well, I've stopped sizzling, but I'm lost in mid-ocean!

Hey! Who's this?

A dolphin! They're supposed to be nearly as clever as little me!

Cleverer, my dear girl!

WATERY WONDERS

The oceans teem with creatures of all kinds of shapes, colours and sizes. Not only fish, squid and shellfish live here, there are also millions of tiny microscopic plants and animals called plankton. Many sea animals rely on plankton for food — blue whales eat four tonnes a day! Some creatures eat other sea animals. Smiffy likes seafood too, but only with chips! Most ocean life dwells near the surface, in the top 180 metres lit by sunlight. Deeper down, the water is always as dark as night.

▽ Most sharks are fierce hunters. They catch fish, squid and even seals in their huge jaws. Sharks have rows of dagger-sharp teeth — when a tooth wears out, it is replaced by another.

If you're so smart, can you get me back to Beanotown?

Heh! What are you doing?

△ Ever heard of a fish that is able to fly? Flying fish can glide 100 m through the air on their wing-like fins!

Yum! Who needs fish 'n' chips when you can have jellyfish 'n' chips?

▽ The blue whale is the biggest mammal alive. A newborn baby weighs a colossal five tonnes and guzzles 450 litres of milk a day!

△ The famous Portuguese man-of-war is not really a jellyfish. It's actually a floating colony of tiny animals. Together they form all the different parts of the man-of-war — from its blue 'sail' right down to the 9 m long tentacles!

Giant clams live on coral reefs. Their shells are big enough to have a bath in.

From the tip of its claws, Japan's giant spider crab is 4 m across. It could open its arms wide enough to hug a hippopotamus!

Ocean sunfish lay 30 million eggs in one go!

Baby seahorses are unusual because they grow in a pouch on their father's belly.

At less than 15 mm long, the dwarf goby is the tiniest fish.

▽ These creatures belong to the vast family of molluscs— there are 120,000 members! All molluscs are soft-bodied, but they form a mixed bunch. They range from mussels to giant clams, and from sea slugs to octopus and squid!

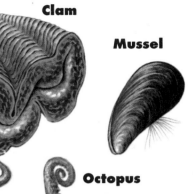

Clam

Mussel

Octopus

△ The weirdest fish live in the dark depths of the ocean. Many of them have huge eyes, fang-like teeth and even glowing fins!

▽ Tread on this stonefish's spines at your peril! It is the most poisonous fish in the world.

◁ The sailfish is the fastest creature in the sea. It can speed through the water at 109 km/h — 12 times faster than any Olympic swimmer.

'Bye, Mr Dolphin!

Home sweet home!

BEANO TOWN BEACH

BUGS ON THE LOOSE

Bugs are the commonest living things. Eight out of ten of all animals are creepy crawlies! You will find them just about everywhere — in the hottest desert and at the top of the highest snow-capped mountain. The Bash Street Kids find it hard to catch these tiny creatures — they can fly, jump, hop and crawl! Some insects are harmful mini-beasts that spread disease and destroy crops. But many are helpful. Others have jobs just like humans. There are insect carpenters, papermakers, nurses and even undertakers!

TEACHER Caught you. But where's Smiffy? I must find him!

◁Dragonflies are the fastest bugs — they can whizz about at a top speed of over 55 km/h when out hunting.

△Disguise is a good way to escape enemies! The tree hopper is a tiny bug with a big prickle on its back. When it sits on a twig, it looks like a thorn!

▽The Queen Alexandra birdwing butterfly is as big as a bird. Its wingspan is a fantastic 28 cm!

CREEPY FACTS

A simple caterpillar has around 3,000 muscles — 6 times as many as a human being.

A flea can jump 130 times its own height. If you were able to do the same, you could easily leap over a fifteen-storey building!

The strands of a spider's web are at least as strong as steel of the same thickness.

Termites are champion builders — they can make mud nests up to 4 times taller than a man.

A tiny midge can beat its wings 62,000 times a second. It is the world's fastest wing-beater.

△This male Goliath beetle of Africa would give Plug's dung beetle a run for his money! More than 10 cm long, this heavyweight would dwarf most other insects.

Wonder if Duncan, my pet Dung Beetle, has any relatives here?

What's that button for?

PRESS

It frees the bugs!

Don't worry!

▷ In 1988 a British blackbird found a worm that was 2 m long. Yet in Africa worms can be twice this size!

▷ The western pygmy is the tiniest butterfly — you would need a magnifying glass to see it properly.

The amazing potter wasp builds tiny clay pots to house its young. In each one the mother wasp lays an egg, pops in a live caterpillar and then seals up the hole. When the baby hatches out, there's a tasty meal waiting!

△ Don't mix spiders up with insects — spiders have eight legs, insects only have six. This monstrous giant tarantula is bigger than your hand!

▽ Women only! Ant colonies are organized around a queen and its female workers. Males only exist to mate with the queens — afterwards they die.

I'll chase 'em back with my fancy dress spider costume!

I found Smiffy. Hope you lot behaved.

Phew! Just made it!

Duncan the Dung Beetle is on the loose. Can you spot him over the next few pages?

25

SCALY AND SCARY

Reptiles are animals with scaly skins. They may look like scary monsters, but most are harmless and shy. Just like Teacher's unruly pupils, many species can blend into their surroundings when they don't want to be seen. Most reptiles lay eggs, but all are cold-blooded. This means that they can't retain their body heat in cold weather. Reptiles need the Sun's warmth before they can muster the energy to run about. When it gets chilly they hibernate, waiting for spring to wake them up.

Crocodile family album

Alligator

Gavial

Caiman

SLITHERY FACTS

The biggest crocodile lives in the rivers of Southeast Asia and is a massive 7 m long. It lies under the water with only its eyes, nostrils and ears showing. Don't mistake it for a log!

The massive South American anaconda is the heaviest snake. It weighs in at 200 kg — as much as a Sumo wrestler!

Russian scientists found a salamander which had been frozen in ice for 90 years. It awoke from its long hibernation when they warmed it up.

Geckos are small lizards with sucker-like pads on their feet. These pads are so strong they can easily run across ceilings!

Snakes can open their mouths wider than their own heads. One reticulated python managed to swallow a 91 kg bear!

Some snakes live in the sea, but they have to surface to breathe air.

△ Crocodiles are caring parents. They carry their babies to the water, safely tucked behind their ferocious jaws.

▷ Turtles are superb swimmers, but they come ashore to lay their eggs. When the babies hatch out, they have a mad scramble to get back to the safety of the water.

◁ The shell of this Aldabra giant tortoise can weigh more than 200 kg. Some live to carry this load around for more than 150 years!

The kids are trying out some camouflage tricks of their own —

Where are they?

▷ Snakes don't smell with their noses — they flick their tongues out to 'taste' scents in the air.

◁ When a rattlesnake shakes its tail, the bony rings at the end click together to make a sound just like a baby's rattle. Heed the warning, Fatty!

▽ The thorny devil lizard is a champion ant-eater. Its darting tongue can pick up 40 ants in a minute — gobbling 1,000 in a single meal.

The chameleon changes colour to match its surroundings, so it can sneak up on prey and hide from enemies. This lizard is able to catch lots of bugs without moving an inch. Using a sticky tongue which is almost as long as its body, it grasps tasty insects and pulls them in!

Grr! Were you able to spot them, readers?

27

BASH STREET BIRDS

Did you know that birds are living dinosaurs? Millions of years ago, some land-living reptiles grew feathers to help them leap from tree to tree. These prehistoric creatures were the ancestors of the bird family. Today there are 9,000 different kinds of birds. They live in every continent — even in the freezing wastes of Antarctica! Not every bird can fly, but all are covered with feathers and lay hard-shelled eggs. The shape of a bird's wings, beak and feet are all specially suited to the way it lives. After watching some of these ingenious animals, Wilfrid will never call anyone a 'bird-brain' again!

▷The albatross has the longest wingspan in the bird world — stretching 3.5 m across, its wings are great for gliding. The hobby hawk has the pointed wings of a quick flier whilst the partridge uses its stubby wings for fast take-offs.

Hobby hawk

Albatross

Partridge

FEATHERY FACTS

An emperor penguin is a fantastic father. It stands alone through the freezing Antarctic winter, keeping its egg warm under a fold of skin.

The bee hummingbird is the smallest bird. At 2 g, it weighs less than half a teaspoon of water.

During World War I, a French carrier pigeon was awarded a medal for bravery.

A cuckoo is the laziest parent — it lays its egg in another bird's nest. When the baby hatches, it pushes the other young birds out to make room for itself.

Swifts spend most of their lives in the air, feeding on the wing. Some even fly through the night.

▷The peregrine falcon folds back its wings and dive-bombs its prey in a screaming 300 km/h dive. This tremendous speed makes it the fastest living animal on Earth.

◁The Arctic tern is the world's greatest traveller. Every year it migrates from the Arctic to the Antarctic and back again. As this small seabird flies the 36,000 km a year from one polar summer to the other, it lives in almost perpetual daylight.

Meet the Bash Street Birds —

See if you can match each bird with the kid who owns it!

BONK!

△ Ostrich eggs are so big, you would have to crack two dozen hens' eggs to make one ostrich-sized omelette.

◁ The tailor bird is an expert homemaker. The mother skilfully uses its beak as a needle and sews leaves together with hair and spider's silk, to make a cosy nest.

△ Ostriches can't fly, but they can run at over 50 km/h!

△ Lovebirds are very affectionate feathery friends! These bright little parrots sit in close pairs fondly preening each other.

A bird has no teeth. Its beak is its knife, fork and spoon. As birds have different tastes in food, each kind has developed a specially shaped bill to make it easier to eat its dinner.

Can you guess how each of these birds uses its beak to catch food?

1   2   3   4   5

ANSWERS: 1 Woodpecker drills for insects, 2 Crossbill cracks nuts, 3 Kestrel tears meat, 4 Spoonbill sieves water for fish, 5 Oystercatcher probes for shellfish

29

FURRY FILM STARS

Most of the animals the Bash Street Kids are watching on the screen belong to the same family, but can you guess which one? Apart from the birds, they are all mammals — warm-blooded creatures covered with some fur or hair. They feed their babies with their own milk and look after them until they can fend for themselves. Mammals form quite a small group in the animal chain, but they make up the most varied and the most intelligent family. Along with monkeys and apes, human beings are mammals too!

Those lions would scare the mice away from Bash Street school!

MAGNIFICENT MAMMALS

Elephants are the heaviest land animals. One elephant can weigh as much as 75 men.

A giraffe's tongue is black and slimy. It uses it to reach high into the trees for leaves, fruit and even thorny twigs.

Many mammals sleep for long periods. Lions sleep for up to 20 hours a day.

A rat can go without water even longer than a camel can!

Beavers' front teeth are so sharp, people once used them as knives.

The smallest mammal is the Kitti's hog-nosed bat from Thailand. The size of a bumblebee, it only weighs 2 g.

Every zebra has its own pattern of stripes which is unique, just like a fingerprint.

The blue whale, the largest of all the world's animals, can weigh as much as 150 cars!

PLANTS FIGHT BACK

If there were no plants, there would be no life on Earth. Plants give off the oxygen that we need to breathe. We know of at least 375,000 different kinds of plants, but there could be just as many undiscovered species growing in remote parts of the world. Some trees can dwarf thirty-storey buildings, while types of plankton are so tiny that 500 can fit on a pinhead. Animals need plants to live, but plants use animals too, to pollinate and spread their seeds. Some even eat meat, as Smiffy is about to find out.

A Venus Fly Trap. What a daft plant!

◁ It would take giant nutcrackers to break open this 18 kg nut. The coco de mer palm comes from the Seychelles — it produces the biggest seeds on Earth.

▽ Yuk! This rafflesia flower from Southeast Asia breaks two records. Not only is it the world's biggest flower, it is also the stinkiest! Each flower can measure a metre across. Rafflesia pongs of rotting meat so it can attract lots of insects to pollinate it.

These plants are all record breakers. The tallest tree ever measured was an Australian eucalyptus (1). Its topmost leaves reached an incredible 132 m high — taller than most skyscrapers! The Californian giant sequoia (2) is the most massive tree. Its trunk can grow wide enough to carve a road through it. The world's longest seaweed is the Pacific giant kelp (3), which stretches up to 60 m long. Giant bamboo (4) is a unique type of grass — it can grow a metre a day!

1   2   3   4

▽ Who is using who? As the hummingbird puts its long beak into a flower to drink the sweet nectar, it picks up pollen on its body and carries it to the next flower. The pollen grains fertilize the waiting flower, making new seeds.

Pitcher plant

▽ These plants eat insects! When a fly lands on the lip of the pitcher plant, it slides into the liquid below and drowns. If it lands on a Venus fly trap, the leaves snap shut and imprison the fly. The sundew uses sticky blobs to stop bugs getting away.

Venus fly trap

Sundew

LEAFY FACTS

Plants suck in water through their roots. The African wild fig has to search so hard for water that its roots are more than 100 m long!

What do tea, cotton, rubber, chewing gum, perfume, cork and chocolate all have in common? Every single one of these products comes from a plant.

The oldest trees are the African bristlecone pines. They are as old as the pyramids of Egypt — this means they have been growing for more than 4,000 years!

Over half of the world's known plants grow in the rainforests, but these regions are disappearing fast. Every second an area as big as a football pitch is destroyed.

This miniature tree is only 40 cm high! It grows in a pot and is kept small by constant pruning. This ancient art comes from Japan — it is called Bonsai.

YEEOW! SLAM!

It should be called a Vedus Doze Trap!

Help! I'm going back where it's safe!

ROARING DINOSAURS

The Earth is a staggering 4,600 million years old. Imagine this vast span of time as just one year. After three months life began in the oceans, but nothing lived on land until eight months later. Dinosaurs roamed the Earth for 11 days and died out a mere five days ago. This would mean that the first human beings appeared only six hours ago and that Roger is less than a tenth of a second old!

▷ Pterosaurs were winged reptiles, the biggest flying animals ever known. This Pteranodon may have used its pointed crest to steer through the air.

▽ Torosaurus had a colossal head — big enough to park a family car on! Its long horns and bony skull protected it during prehistoric battles.

△ Tyrannosaurus rex was the scariest dinosaur. Its huge jaws were packed with dagger-like teeth — each 15 cm long!

△ Fossils show that dinosaurs had scaly skin, but what colour were they? Some may have been covered with pink spots or even black and red stripes!

WEIRD AND WONDERFUL

Four-legged animals probably developed from fish that left the water to 'walk' on their fins!

The biggest insects ever were giant dragonflies that lived 350 million years ago. They had a wingspan as big as a pigeon's.

Scientists can work out how fast a dinosaur ran by

looking at its skeleton and at its footprints fossilized in the rock.

The longest known dinosaur footprint was over 136 cm — the size of a dining table.

I'm going to show you some of my dodging ancestors!

This is the easy way to clean your cave!

▽Fancy a mouth-watering mammoth burger? Although the last of these prehistoric creatures died out 20,000 years ago, mammoth bodies have been found deep frozen in the ice — the meat still good enough to eat!

△Early mammals were the size of rats or mice and probably fed on insects. Larger mammals didn't appear until the dinosaurs had died out, over 65 million years ago!

The first people lived in caves. They painted the animals they hunted straight onto rock and probably thought that they brought good luck. The oldest cave paintings were done over 20,000 years ago, but don't try it on your bedroom walls!

Bone-headed dinosaurs had skulls 23 cm thick — as solid as a brick wall.

Brachiosaurus was the largest land animal that ever lived. This plant-eating giant stretched

further than 2 buses parked end to end!

Prehistoric horses were no larger than a common cat.

Cavemen wore their furs inside out. It may have

itched, but they were much warmer that way!

So few people lived in the Stone Age that most humans probably only saw 25 to 50 other people in their entire lives.

TOWERING TOMBS

The Ancient Egyptian civilization thrived for over 3,000 years. The Egyptians believed in life after death and were buried with all the belongings they thought they'd need in the afterlife. They even had their pet dogs and cats mummified and buried with them, so watch out Gnasher! The pyramids are the stone tombs of Egypt's kings — the pharaohs. These ancient monuments stand on the banks of the river Nile. Some are over 4,500 years old!

△ This fabulous golden mask was made for Tutankhamun, an Egyptian king who died at the age of 18. His great tomb lay hidden with its priceless treasure untouched until it was finally discovered in 1922.

EGYPTIAN FACTS

It is said that the tomb of Tutankhamun carried a curse. Several people died mysteriously after they had visited the chamber.

The Egyptians made the first kind of paper from reeds called papyrus.

Egyptian women liked make-up. They wore lipstick and plucked their eyebrows. They even used

to colour their nails, palms and the soles of their feet.

False burial chambers and secret passages were built into the pyramids to fool robbers trying to plunder the tombs of the pharaohs.

The Egyptians used a form of picture writing called hieroglyphics. Each sign was a little picture or symbol standing for a letter, or sometimes a syllable. Can you work out the Beano picture code?

▽ All of the pyramids were built by hand! The Egyptians had no iron tools or machinery to help them. They probably dragged the massive blocks of stone into place on sledges run on specially built ramps. These gigantic tombs show that the Egyptians were very skilful architects and builders — although no one knows why the pyramids were shaped this way.

Egyptians paid vast sums of money to have their bodies properly preserved. Trained undertakers treated the body with chemicals and wrapped it in tight bandages to keep it in shape.

The last Egyptian pharaoh was a Greek woman — Queen Cleopatra.

The only source of water in Egypt is the river Nile. When it flooded each year, peasants stopped farming

and spent a few months building pyramids instead.

Tombs of the later pharaohs were built by criminals or prisoners of war. They were treated well and given cottages to

live in with their families near the building site.

When a dead person was mummified, only the heart was left inside the body. The brain was hooked out through the nose!

ANSWER: If you want to dodge puzzling, answer's at foot of page!

ROGER THE GREAT

Step back 2,000 years and look at the ancient civilizations of Greece and Rome. At the height of the Greek empire, King Alexander the Great conquered an immense kingdom, spreading ideas on government, philosophy and art. Then came the great age of the Romans, who controlled a vast realm with their strong and disciplined army. Both nations were advanced thinkers and skilful engineers — their plumbing systems alone would rival those in modern-day Beanotown!

▷The Greeks invented the idea of democracy — government by the people. Men in Athens could vote in trials, using metal discs to declare guilty or not guilty.

◁The first Olympic Games were held in Greece in 776 BC. Only men were allowed to compete and they performed naked!

Greek plays were acted in colossal open-air theatres. All the parts were played by men who wore masks to identify the different characters. Some theatres seated over 10,000 people and are still used today.

▽Ancient Greece had an outstanding navy. One ferocious sea battle took place in 480 BC against the Persians. The Greeks forced their enemies to retreat, even though the Persians had three times as many ships!

ANCIENT ANTICS

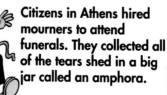

Ever heard of Socrates, Plato or Aristotle? They were 3 of the world's greatest thinkers, all of them Ancient Greeks.

Citizens in Athens hired mourners to attend funerals. They collected all of the tears shed in a big jar called an amphora.

The early Olympic games included musical and literary competitions, as well as running, javelin throwing and gymnastics.

The Greeks worshipped many gods — beings that quarrelled and fell in love just like people.

40

My Roman ancestor was a great gladiator!

HO HO!

I surrenderus!

HA HA!

TICKLE!

▷ A Roman soldier had to be really strong. His heavy armour, helmet, shield and weapons weighed nearly 30 kg! In a basket on his back he also had a pick, a saw, an axe and three days' food.

▽ The bloodthirsty emperors built amphitheatres where they watched wild animals or gladiators fight each other to death. The most popular sports included chariot races and throwing Christians to packs of starving lions.

Most Roman towns had public baths with indoor pools and saunas — even jacuzzis! Water was brought down from the hills through aqueducts and pipes.

▽ The Romans had fast food takeaways 2,000 years before America re-invented them!

MAXIMUS

STUFFED DORMICE XVIII LIRA

Rome's chariot-racing stadium, the Circus Maximus, was 550 m long by 180 m wide. The stands could hold up to 250,000 spectators — more than a quarter of the city's population!

Roman roads were built to move the army around quickly. Everyone else had to clear the streets when the troops came along.

The rich hosted parties that went on for days. People lounged on couches, drinking wine and eating until they were sick. They even had a special room called a vomitorium!

A favourite Roman party dish was stuffed dormice.

PILLAGING PIRATES

Check out Roger the Viking!

PROD!

Nothing was more terrifying in the AD 800s than the sight of Viking longboats making for the shore. These Norse raiders killed the people and stole their gold, often burning villages behind them! The Vikings were originally farmers and merchants from Scandinavia who set sail in search of better farmland and wealth. But Roger's dodging ancestors are most famous for being fearless adventurers. They traded goods around the world and settled throughout Europe — even in the freezing climes of Iceland! They were also the first Europeans to reach North America. In 1003 Leif Ericson landed in Newfoundland, 500 years before Columbus!

BACK IN TIME

Sword handle

Stick handle

Not all Vikings were savage warriors — many were highly skilled craftsmen. They made attractive jewellery and leather clothing. They also carved iron and horn into ornate sword handles and spearheads.

Silver bangle

Spearhead

Leather ice skate

NORSE FACTS

In Scandinavia the word Viking meant pirate or warrior. The Vikings were also known as Norsemen, Northmen or Danes.

The Vikings ate seagulls, polar bears, walruses, horses, seaweed — and tonnes of fish!

The Danes believed that if they died in battle, they would go to a place called

Valhalla, where they would fight all day and feast all night.

The Scandinavians had no buttons or zips. They used carved brooches to hold their clothes together.

42

▽ The success of the Vikings rested on the design of their longboats. These wooden ships were narrow and flat-bottomed. This meant they could be rowed up rivers as well as sailed across the sea!

Famous Viking warriors were buried in their longboats. Sometimes animals and slaves were buried with them.

Vikings had names like Dennis the Menace. They

included Olaf the Stout, Asgot the Clumsy, Ivar the Boneless, Ragnar Hairy Breeches and Harold Bluetooth.

The Althing was the world's first parliament,

held in Iceland in AD 930. Each Viking community had its own Althing.

The Vikings told each other long stories called sagas which weren't written down for years and years.

THE BEANO TAPESTRY

In 1066 William the Conqueror invaded England and became its first Norman king. He was so proud of his victory that a fabulous 70 metre long tapestry was sewn to tell the story. There are 72 scenes in the Bayeux tapestry, just like the ones being acted out by the Beano gang. For the next 500 years England was controlled by wealthy noblemen who lived in great castles. These lords collected taxes and maintained an army of knights, while the peasants toiled in the fields to support them.

Fatty would have loved a medieval feast! The menu included whole pigs, roast swans and vast jellies moulded like castles. Everyone had their own knife but ate mainly with their fingers. All the food was served on big slices of bread called trenchers, which the castle servants got to eat afterwards.

MEDIEVAL FACTS

William of Normandy wanted a count of everything he had conquered. The Domesday Book is a precise record of all the land, cattle and people he had gained.

At this time it was thought that the world was flat and that the Sun and stars moved around the Earth!

If a castle was attacked, people tipped vats of boiling oil over the walls to stop invaders getting in.

There was usually only one oven in a medieval village — at the local baker's. Women had to take their pies there to be cooked.

There were few toilets in the Middle Ages. People used a pot and flung the smelly contents into the street!

WARS AND WONDERS

Between the years 1300 and 1800 Europeans began to explore new ideas and new lands. Ships sailed into the unknown, reaching North and South America, Australia and distant New Zealand. During these exciting times people took a revived interest in learning and art. The reign of Queen Elizabeth I was a prosperous time for England. But let's hope Roger stays out of trouble — criminals were beheaded at public executions!

BACK IN TIME

◁ When Columbus reached a group of islands in 1492, he thought he had found a new route to India across the Atlantic Ocean. He called them the West Indies, but in fact they were the Caribbean Islands off the coast of North America. He never realized his mistake!

Italy was the centre of the Renaissance, a 'rebirth' in learning and art in the 1500s. Michelangelo was one of its greatest leaders. He excelled as a painter, architect and sculptor — skilled at portraying human figures in a realistic way. When Michelangelo carved this statue of Moses, he even added veins and muscles in the arms and legs.

◁ Elizabeth I was so powerful that her 45-year reign was called the Elizabethan Age! Here she is encouraging her troops to defend England against a massive armada of Spanish warships. The English vessels were much smaller and speedier than the Spanish fleet, which they defeated in 1588.

RENAISSANCE FACTS

Leonardo da Vinci was a great engineer as well as an outstanding artist. He designed a helicopter, aeroplane and submarine!

Sir Francis Drake was the most famous of Queen Elizabeth I's sea captains. Stories say he was playing bowls when the Spanish Armada attacked, but he vowed to finish his game before he went to war.

Early visitors to America and Asia brought new products back to Europe, including potatoes, sugar, exotic spices and apricots!

Shakespeare died on his birthday, 23 April, 1616.

How kind, Sir Roger!

Kind? It was my jacket!

△ Charles I believed that God had made him king, but Parliament disagreed. They thought he was a corrupt man. Fighting broke out between the two sides — the last civil war in English history. It ended in 1649 when Charles was beheaded.

△ Before the British captured New York in North America in 1664, Dutch settlers had proudly named it New Amsterdam!

In 1666 a great fire ripped through the heart of London, destroying everything in its path. Most of the buildings were wooden, so the fire quickly spread. People took to the river Thames to escape the flames.

▷ In 1789 many people in Paris were jobless and hungry. On July 14th, after the price of bread had been doubled, an angry mob stormed the Bastille prison. The French Revolution had just begun. Anyone who was considered an enemy of the revolution was beheaded on the guillotine.

Elizabeth I was thought to be very clean — she had 4 baths a year, whether she needed them or not!

By the way, Roger is wrong about Sir Walter Raleigh letting Queen

Elizabeth I walk on his cloak. That story was made up by an historian called Thomas Fuller!

It took 35 years for Sir Christopher Wren to build the new St Paul's Cathedral.

The original building was destroyed in the Great Fire.

More than half of all taxes the French people paid to King Louis XIV were spent on building his sumptuous palace at Versailles.

EMPIRES AND INVENTIONS

Queen Victoria's reign lasted 63 years — the longest rule in British history. During this amazing age the telephone, camera and car were invented. Trains steamed across the continents for the first time. Yet the poorest people had to pay a high price for so much progress. They lived in city slums, labouring long hours in factories. Many escaped the misery of Europe and settled across North America in search of new land to farm. Let's hope they don't get ambushed by Dennis!

△ In 1856, Queen Victoria introduced the Victoria Cross — the highest military decoration to be awarded in Britain and the Commonwealth. Less than 1,500 people have received this great honour.

▽ Charles Dickens was a very popular English author. Several of his stories deal with orphans and poor children, describing the harsh conditions they suffered in Victorian England. These Beano kids have dressed up as famous Dickens' characters — can you recognize them?

American Thomas Edison was probably the greatest inventor in history. As a boy he had only three months of schooling, yet he was a genius! He changed the lives of millions of people with such inventions as the electric light bulb, the gramophone, and over 1,000 other useful things!

Gramophone

Light bulb

▷ Fancy some work Roger? Children as young as eight were sent out to work in factories and coal mines. In 1833, however, a law was passed which said that children under 13 could 'only' work a 48-hour week!

VICTORIAN FACTS

Even little girls had to wear corsets and crinolines in Victorian times. The corsets were pulled so tight, many grew up deformed.

More soldiers died from infections caught in army hospitals than at the battle of Waterloo in 1815.

The poor had to live in slums. Often 12 or more shared a room with just 4 beds. The only tap was a stand-pipe in the street!

London's river Thames was a huge sewer! Drains just emptied straight into it. But it was also London's main source of drinking water.

My Victorian ancestor's dodges didn't always work!

Can't go to school, Miss Nightingale! I've got spots!

Can't fool me! Those spots are just soot!

Ah, well! Good try!

△ Florence Nightingale became a legend during the Crimean War in 1854. She saved hundreds of lives by improving the terrible conditions in army hospitals that lacked food, beds and medicine. After the war her methods were used worldwide.

◁ In 1859 Victorian society was outraged by Charles Darwin's theory that human beings had evolved from apes. Most people believed that nothing had changed since God created Adam and Eve.

▷ In the 1800s, toys like this car and teddy bear were mass-produced in factories for the first time.

◁ David Livingstone was the first European to sight the Victoria Falls in South Africa, which he named after Queen Victoria.

In 1840 the British Post Office issued the 'Penny Black'. This was the first postage stamp that had to be prepaid by the sender.

When Victoria's husband, Prince Albert, died in

1861 the queen went into mourning — and hiding. She refused to appear in public for 7 years.

The great age of the Wild West only lasted 20 years! By 1890, new trains and

fencing meant that cattle didn't need to be tended by cowboys anymore.

Think you don't get enough pocket money? Some Victorians earnt as little as 15p for a week's work!

BACK TO THE FUTURE

Roger is very glad that he lives in the 20th century. Better medicines, central heating, television and cheaper food and clothes make life more comfortable and entertaining than ever before. There are more and more people alive to enjoy this progress, but not everyone is having a good time. Millions have been killed by wars and famines. Roger wonders if the next century will be a better one for everybody.

▽Bombs and other weapons have made warfare even more deadly. Millions of soldiers lost their lives in the trenches of World War I. During World War II thousands of innocent civilians were also killed. Today, worldwide conflict continues the bloodshed.

▷'Erbert and Toots are doing the Charleston, a popular dance of the 1920s. People partied the nights away, trying to forget the horror of World War I.

This is the great picture upon which the famous comedian has worked a whole year.

6 reels of Joy.

Charles Chaplin in "THE KID"

◁People used to flock to the cinema to see their favourite Hollywood stars on screen! Charlie Chaplin acted in many silent black and white films, before colour and 'talkies' came into use.

▽Almost every country in the world today has someone to represent them at the United Nations. Together they try to solve the problems of famine, poverty and war. The UN is based in New York, USA.

20TH CENTURY FACTS

Women had to fight for the right to vote in the early 1900s. Some people said they might as well give the vote to horses and dogs!

World War I was often described as 'the war to end all wars' — some hope!

When London was bombed during World War II, 200,000 people

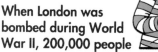

slept in the Underground for safety.

For nearly 30 years a wall split Germany's capital, Berlin, in half. Anyone trying to escape from East to West Berlin was shot.

▽ The Eurotunnel links England and France by rail, deep under the English Channel. It was carved out by tunnel-boring machines that weighed 1,300 tonnes each! If all the earth and rubble from the tunnel were stacked up in a great pile, it would be as tall as the Eiffel Tower!

▷ In the last 20 years, computers have taken over — in offices, banks and even our homes. Computers can do millions of calculations in seconds. Just one microchip can store 160 pages of information!

This is Hong Kong — a city-state built on a small island off China. It is one of the world's most crowded places. As the Earth gets more populated, land becomes more expensive. With no room on the ground, huge skyscrapers serve as offices, flats and hotels.

In 1961 Mrs Bandaranaike of Sri Lanka became the first woman to be elected leader of a country.

Russian scientists launched a satellite in space in 1957 — starting the race with

the USA to land the first man on the Moon. But the USA won in 1969!

The largest TV audience ever saw Live Aid in 1985, raising millions of pounds for famine victims in Ethiopia.

By the year 2000 there will probably be 6,000 million people on Earth. If the extra 500 million people alive in 2000 joined hands they could form a vast chain — long enough to go round the world 20 times!

ATOMIC SPIN

Atoms are so incredibly small that even the most powerful microscopes cannot show them to us, yet they are the building blocks of the Universe. They link together to make all the different substances in the world — wood, iron, air, salt, skin, even the Bash Street Kids! Everything on Earth is made of atoms, but what are atoms made of? They are composed of even smaller particles — electrons that spin around a centre of minute protons and neutrons. Atoms link together with other atoms to form molecules.

What do ice, water and steam have in common? They are all forms of water. When water gets cold enough it freezes into solid ice. When it heats up it turns into steam. Most substances can exist as a solid, liquid or gas and change state when cooled or heated. In steam, the hot water molecules whizz around really quickly, often bumping into each other — just like the Bash Street Kids!

MINIATURE FACTS

Atoms are so small, it takes a million billion of them just to make a speck of dust.

The Greek philosopher Democritus said that an atom was the smallest uncuttable particle. It took nearly 3,000 years for scientists to split an atom and prove him wrong.

The centre, or nucleus of an atom is made up of protons and neutrons. But they may be made of even tinier particles called quarks.

Electrons spin so fantastically fast around the nucleus, they make billions of orbits within just a millionth of a second.

We're all made up of atoms and molecules!

Let's act like atoms!

BOUNCE

BOING

Phew! Don't atoms ever get tired?

▽ This model shows a molecule magnified billions of times. The round balls are the atoms. Some molecules have just two atoms, but others have many thousands. This molecule belongs to a crystal because its atoms are arranged in regular patterns.

▷ Atoms are unbelievably tiny. If an atom were the size of your fingernail, then your hand would be big enough to grasp the Earth!

INVISIBLE ENERGY

You can't see energy, but it is everywhere. Without it there would be no machines, no light or sound and no movement. The Bash Street Kids would grind to a halt without food energy to keep their bodies running. Energy makes things happen. Every moving thing has a type of energy called kinetic energy — even a falling water bomb! Radiant energy from the Sun gives us most of our energy on Earth. Coal, oil and gas were all formed from the remains of plants and animals that depended on the Sun's light and warmth.

▽ Most of the energy we use on Earth comes from the Sun. Sunlight makes plants grow, then plants provide food for animals and people. But most of the energy beamed to Earth from the Sun bounces back into space. If we could trap it all, we could get enough in just one minute to provide the world with all the energy it needs for a day!

▷ Coal, oil and gas are stores of energy. These fossil fuels are mined from below the ground and burnt to produce heat, light and power.

△ Vast amounts of energy get wasted. Petrol is used in cars, but they only use a quarter of the energy available. The rest is lost as heat!

◁ Energy is the world's greatest form-changer. It cannot be created or destroyed, but it is constantly changing from one form to another. Hairdryers turn electrical energy into heat energy and kinetic energy. In other words, they blow hot air!

△ The energy we get from food is stored inside our bodies. We use it in everything we do — breathing, walking and playing games.

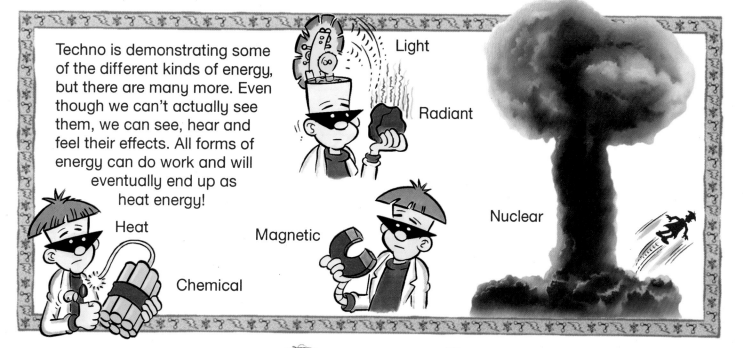

Techno is demonstrating some of the different kinds of energy, but there are many more. Even though we can't actually see them, we can see, hear and feel their effects. All forms of energy can do work and will eventually end up as heat energy!

Light

Radiant

Heat

Magnetic

Nuclear

Chemical

▽Oil is such a valuable energy source it is sometimes called 'black gold'. But fossil fuels will soon run out — oil reserves may only last another 30 years! To solve the problem, we must investigate other sources of energy such as wind and solar power.

◁Recycling saves energy and raw materials. It takes a great deal of energy to extract new aluminium for drinks cans — recycling saves this extra waste and pollution. Used glass, metal and paper can all be recycled.

△Each recycled drinks can saves 95 per cent of the energy needed to make a new one!

This is potential energy!

That was kinetic energy!

ELECTRO TECHNO

DISCOVER SCIENCE

Electricity is a silent, invisible form of energy that is stored in electrons — the tiny particles inside atoms. If electrons collect in one place, static electricity builds up. But if they move in a line, an electric current is produced. Magnetism is closely related to electricity. A magnet is a piece of metal that can attract some other objects towards it. It can also be converted into an electric current. So watch out Kids — you've magnetized Techno, but electric sparks could soon be flying!

▽A force is pulling these two magnets together. But if you turned one of them round, you could not even get the ends to touch! The ends of the magnets have different charges, called north and south poles. The north pole of one magnet attracts the south pole of the other magnet. Yet two north poles or two south poles will always push each other apart.

▽You can change a lump of iron into a powerful magnet by wrapping it in a coil of wire and connecting it up to a battery. Electromagnets only work when the electric current is turned on.

▽As electromagnets attract iron and steel, they can be used to pick up heavy pieces of metal. This huge electromagnet lifts scrapped cars. The driver drops the tangled metal by simply switching off the current!

I'm going to attract you with this magnet, Danny!

Magnets only attract metal objects, Smiffy!

Why did I tell them that?

△ This power station burns fossil fuels to power the generator blades that produce electricity. But some stations use nuclear energy to run generators. Hydroelectric plants rely on water power to create electricity.

△ Electricity can be produced in nature. A flash of lightning is a huge spark in the atmosphere, as powerful as 50 million batteries! Lightning conductors channel the electricity harmlessly into the ground.

▷ This industrial robot moves according to instructions from its electronic circuits. These are devices that control the flow of electric current. Whole circuits can be made small enough to fit on a tiny silicon chip!

What happens when you rub a balloon against your jersey or hair and then let it go? Try it and see. If you hold the balloon near a wall, it sticks as if it was glued on! Electrons pass from the jersey onto the balloon, charging it with static electricity.

▷ This arc welder is using an electric current to melt and join two pieces of metal without even touching them! The current passes through the air, producing an arc of intense heat and light, hot enough to melt and join the metals.

SOUNDS AMAZING

Unlike light, sound can travel around corners and even through metal and brick walls! All sounds are made by something vibrating. Put your fingers on your throat and make a noise. Can you feel your vocal chords quivering? Pluck a guitar string and you will see and hear it vibrating. The air around it vibrates too and carries the sound to your ears. The Mexican wave the Bash Street Kids are making passes along the line, just like a sound wave. The loudness of the sound depends on the height of the wave.

1,000 Hertz

70 60 50 40 30 20 10

△ Many sounds are either too high or too low for our ears. Gnasher is able to hear high-pitched sounds that Dennis can't. Gnasher's enemy, the cat, can hear even higher squeaks than that! Pitch is measured in Hertz.

Who knows anything about waves?

I do!

▽ Have you ever heard a jet plane long after you've seen it fly overhead? That's because it's flying faster than the speed of sound! Sound travels at 1,224 km/h.

▽ Sounds bounce back from solid objects. This mini-sub is recording the location of a shipwreck. An echo-sounding device called sonar sends sound waves out towards the wreck. The time the echo takes to come back tells the submarine where the ship is lying.

◁ As Concorde hits supersonic speed it flies through a barrier of sound waves, making a loud bang called a sonic boom.

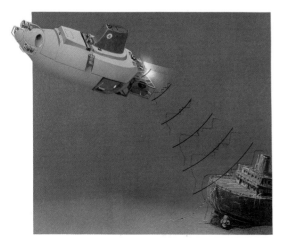

▷ Toots' singing has broken the wine glass! This rare operatic accident has taken place because Toots hit a note that made the glass vibrate so much it shattered — not because her singing is so terrible!

60

NOISY FACTS

The loudness of a sound is measured in decibels (dB). A sound of more than 145 dB can deafen you, over 165 dB can kill you.

No one heard the loudest bang on Earth. Scientists think that a giant meteor hit the ground 65 million years ago in what is now the West Indies. No people were alive then, but dinosaurs living in what is now Britain would have heard the deafening bang!

Space is silent because there is nothing to carry the sound waves. Apart from a few atoms, space is almost a vacuum.

Sound travels 200,000 times slower than light. That's why you see a flash of lightning before you hear the thunder, even though they happen at the same time.

▽ How fast does sound travel? It depends on what it is travelling through. Surprisingly, sound vibrations can travel faster and further through water than through air. This is why porpoises and whales up to 800 km apart can hear each other's songs.

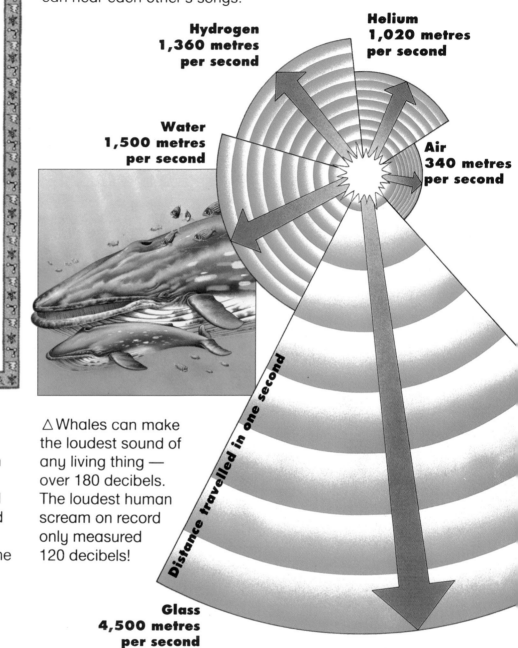

**Hydrogen
1,360 metres
per second**

**Helium
1,020 metres
per second**

**Water
1,500 metres
per second**

**Air
340 metres
per second**

Distance travelled in one second

**Glass
4,500 metres
per second**

◁ The loudest engine noise ever recorded was that of the Saturn space rocket being launched. It measured 210 decibels — loud enough to deafen and even kill anyone standing nearby, unless they were wearing earmuffs.

△ Whales can make the loudest sound of any living thing — over 180 decibels. The loudest human scream on record only measured 120 decibels!

That's the shape of a sound wave!

It's a Mexican wave, too!

LIGHT FANTASTIC

Light travels faster than anything else in the Universe and unlike sound, it can travel through space. It takes just eight minutes for the light from the Sun to reach us here on Earth. Light always travels in straight lines. When it hits an object, some of the light is absorbed, but most of it bounces off. You can see the things around you because some of the light which bounces off them reaches your eyes. But can you always believe what you see? Spotty and Plug look strange, but not as strange as the fairground mirrors show!

Nothing is faster than the speed of light!

▽ A rainbow shows all the colours that are in sunlight. Look for a rainbow when the Sun is behind you and it is raining in front. The light is split into seven separate colours as it passes through the drops of rain.

▽ This straw looks as if it is broken in two, but it isn't. This effect is called refraction. Light rays change speed as they pass from air into water, making them bend. This means that our view of the straw is bent too.

▽ Curved mirrors show crazy reflections! When you look in a flat mirror the light bounces straight back to you. But the light from these mirrors bounces off in all directions, giving a distorted image.

▽ The stars are so many million kilometres away it is easier to measure the distance using light. Light travels 300,000 km in just one second! In one year it travels an amazing 9.5 million million km — or one light year.

▷ Light from the nearest star to the Sun takes 4.2 years to reach us here on Earth!

△ Can you believe that a beam of light could be so powerful that it could bore through rock? This special kind of light is called a laser — a straight, narrow beam of pure light, whose rays hardly spread out at all. Lasers can cut metal, carry telephone calls and even play compact discs! The laser above is being used to check if a tunnel is straight.

White light is made up of the seven colours of the rainbow. Hard to believe? Divide a circle of card into seven sections and colour in each slice with one of the rainbow colours. Push a pencil through the centre and spin it. If it spins fast enough you will see all the colours blend together and disappear into white!

MAGIC MIXTURES

Chemistry is like magic. It can make some things disappear and it can change one thing into another. Everything you can see around you is composed of chemical substances called elements. They combine together to make all the millions of different things in the world — metal, water, wood, soil, leaves, plastic, glass and so on. Chemists experiment with different substances and make new ones. Thanks to chemists we have antibiotics, vitamins, fertilizers, dyes, rubbers and plastics. But if Techno has really found a way of changing coal into diamonds he'll become a millionaire!

1 Hydrogen H

20 Calcium Ca

19 Potassium K

△ Hydrogen, potassium and calcium are all elements. There are 92 elements known in nature, but chemists have made 11 more artificially. An element has only one kind of atom and is recorded in a special list called the Periodic Table. The number shows how many electrons each atom has.

Observe this piece of coal!

Such is my android power . . .

▷ Diamonds and pencil lead are both forms of pure carbon. The atoms in a diamond form a strong lattice framework — the hardest substance known. Yet graphite is one of the softest because its atoms are arranged in layers.

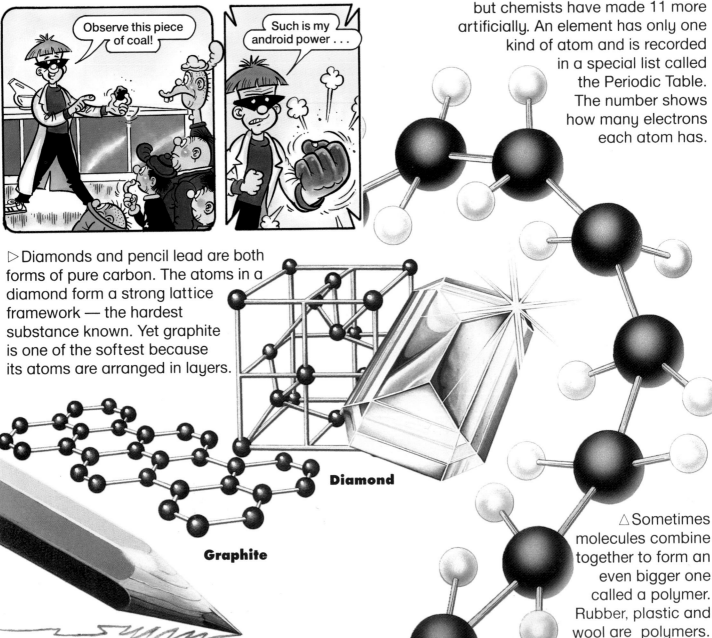

Diamond

Graphite

△ Sometimes molecules combine together to form an even bigger one called a polymer. Rubber, plastic and wool are polymers.

64

Our bodies contain many chemicals. Teacher has been coloured in to show how much of which chemical elements make up his body. It's a surprising mixture — more than half the atoms in his body are oxygen. And if the carbon were pure, there would be enough to fill 3,000 pencils!

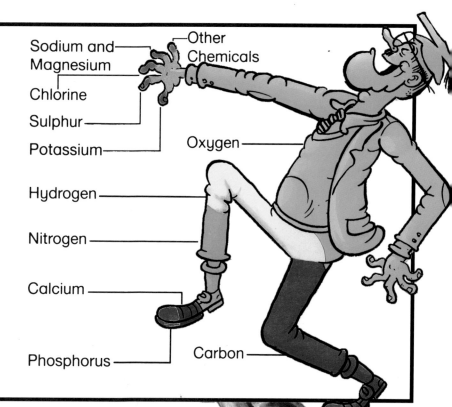

Sodium and Magnesium
Other Chemicals
Chlorine
Sulphur
Potassium
Oxygen
Hydrogen
Nitrogen
Calcium
Phosphorus
Carbon

65%		2%	
18%		2%	
9%		1%	
3%			

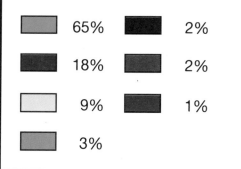

CHEMICAL FACTS

Check what your clothes are made of. Nylon, polyester, viscose and acrylic are all polymers.

Water is actually a molecule made up of 2 atoms of hydrogen and 1 atom of oxygen.

People have been making use of chemical reactions to smelt metal and make glass for more than 5,000 years!

There is enough iron in an adult's body to make a nail 15 cm long.

▽If you drop sugar into a warm cup of tea and stir it, the sugar disappears. The molecules of sugar have simply spread out and slotted in between the molecules of water. However, if you left the tea to evaporate, the sugar would reappear as the tea faded away!

▷No amount of chemistry will turn rusty iron or steel back into pure metal. Oxygen in the air has combined with the iron to make iron oxide — rust. Chemical reactions like this can't be reversed.

65

MENACE ON WHEELS

Without wheels there'd be no carts, cars, trains or bicycles — no way, in fact, to get about on land except walking or riding a horse. For thousands of years wheeled vehicles were mainly used to carry heavy weights. The roads were so rough and slow, few people travelled far from home. Trains, and then cars, changed all that. Dennis has progressed from his own 'early car' to a menacemobile! But he is not alone. So many cars now clog the roads that each one, in its own way, is a menacemobile.

▽ The first wheels were cut from tree trunks. People bumped along on wooden wheels for thousands of years. Just 100 years ago, John Boyd Dunlop invented air-filled rubber tyres. Comfort at last!

Dennis's changing means of transport —

Hobby horse

△ The first bicycle, called a hobby horse, had no pedals. Later came the penny-farthing which was fast, but you had to keep pedalling, or you'd fall off!

Penny-farthing bicycle

▷ People were amazed when the first motor cars appeared on the streets 100 years ago. They called them 'horseless carriages' and even tried to get them banned.

▽ Until 1896 a law ruled in Britain that someone had to walk in front of every car on the road, waving a red flag to warn others that it was coming.

△ The world's longest car has 26 wheels. Three of them parked end to end would stretch the length of a football pitch! But there is only one of these cars. It was built in California, USA and includes an oven, a sink, a refrigerator, four telephones and a 3.6 m swimming pool!

MOVING FACTS

In China, bicycles are the most popular form of transport. There are thought to be 210 million bikes — 1 for every 5 people!

The first motorcycle with a petrol engine was built in 1885. Most of it was carved from wood.

The most popular car ever made is the Volkswagon Beetle. Over 21 million vehicles have been produced throughout the world.

The longest train on record stretched 7 km. It pulled 600 wagons in South Africa in 1989!

▷ This puffing, clanking machine was the world's first working steam locomotive! It made its first run in 1804.

◁ Big Boys were the biggest steam locomotives. When they were used in the 1940s, they burnt over 2,200 sacks of coal every hour!

Japanese Bullet

▷ It is hard to say which is the world's fastest passenger train — the Japanese Bullet or the French TGV. Both regularly travel at over 300 km/h.

French TGV

△ This huge, powerful locomotive is pulling a long string of freight wagons across the United States. The 'cow catcher' at the front clears the line ahead of branches, stones and, if necessary, cows!

67

FLYING AND FLOATING

What is the easiest way to make a long journey? The answer, of course, is to go by plane. But before flying was possible, the answer was to travel by sea. In 1521 Ferdinand Magellan led the first expedition around the world. He died on route, but it took his crew three years! In 1993 five men sailed around the globe in just 79 days. Compare this to the supersonic airliner Concorde, that took just 32 hours to complete the same journey! Ships and aircraft are getting faster all the time. But for people like Dennis, the biggest attraction of boats and planes is just getting away from firm land.

△ This jet-powered hydroplane is the fastest ship ever built. In 1977 it skimmed over the water at an amazing 556 km/h!

GLIDING FACTS

Submarines travel under the sea. They have even ventured under the thick ice of the Arctic Ocean.

In 1783, the first hot-air balloon took off with 3 passengers — a duck, a sheep and a cockerel! Soon after this test flight, 2 Frenchmen became the first people to fly.

The 294 m long QE2 is one of the most luxurious liners on Earth. It takes a vast crew of 1,000 to serve the 1,900 passengers on board.

Concorde heats up so much in flight that its body stretches, often by as much as 28 cm!

◁ The *Essex* was a large merchant ship called an East Indiaman, especially built in the 1600s to carry cargo to India and the Far East. It had more sails than any other ship in history. The complete set totalled 63, with 21 sails on the main mast alone!

▽ Supertankers are the world's biggest ships. They dwarf the great ships of the past and make most of today's seacraft look tiny. Four football pitches could fit on a supertanker's deck with room to spare!

Brothers Orville and Wilbur Wright were two Americans who built and flew the first ever successful petrol-engined aeroplane — *Flyer 1*. In 1903, the plane stayed in the air for 12 seconds and flew 37 m!

▽America's SR-71 Blackbird is officially the fastest aeroplane in service. It can fly at over 3,000 km/h, taking aerial photographs of the land and sea below.

▽Most fast jets need long runways to take-off and land, but the Harrier fighter plane can rise vertically into the air and then land on the spot. That's how it earned the nickname 'jump jet'.

△Microlights are the lightest and smallest aircraft. There is only room for the pilot!

FROM HEAD TO TOE

Your body is like a wonderful machine with thousands of separate parts. Each part has a special job to do. Like machines, bodies need fuel to work. This fuel is provided by food, which the body turns into energy. But your body can do more than any other machine because it can grow, rebuild itself and fight disease. Although they look different, Dennis and Gnasher have similar bodies — they both have bones, muscles, a heart and stomach. Yet Dennis has an advantage. With a bigger brain he can speak, think, laugh and understand ideas that mean nothing to Gnasher.

Gnasher thinks dogs are better than people!

▷No wonder this skeleton is grinning. If we didn't have bones we would just be shapeless blobs! Over 200 bones shape your body and protect your insides. The smallest one is in the ear. It is only about 2.5 mm long!

FLESHY FACTS

It takes up to 24 hours for food to pass right through your body.

You shed a complete layer of skin about every 3 weeks. Most house dust is actually dead skin.

An average person eats at least 50 tonnes of food and drinks 42,000 litres of liquid in a lifetime.

Ear wax keeps your ears clean! It traps dirt and dust and slowly pushes it out.

A sneeze is just a sudden explosion of air from the lungs. It can make air rocket out of the nose at up to 165 km/h!

If your lungs were laid out flat they would cover an area as big as a tennis court.

If you hold a shell to your ear, it isn't the sea that you hear but the sound of the blood flowing around inside your head.

When you walk your body uses 200 different muscles.

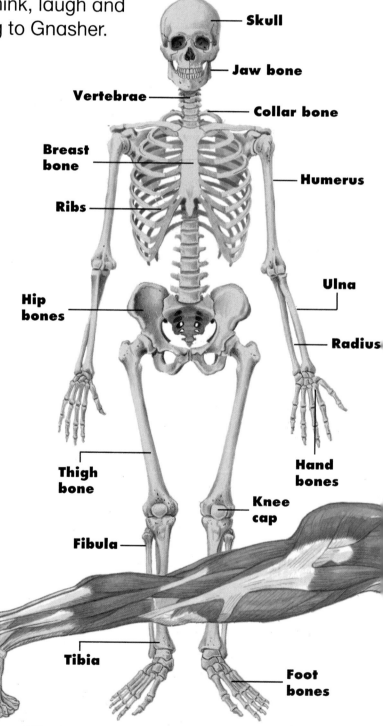

Skull
Jaw bone
Vertebrae
Collar bone
Breast bone
Humerus
Ribs
Ulna
Hip bones
Radius
Thigh bone
Hand bones
Knee cap
Fibula
Tibia
Foot bones

△Did you know your face is full of muscles? Frowning uses 40 different muscles, but smiling uses just 15. So keep smiling!

▽The brain is your control centre, processing information from every part of the body. Different parts of the brain are used for different tasks. Most thinking is done in the front of the brain, whereas sight is controlled from the back!

▷Thousands of millions of nerves stretch all over your body. They carry messages to and from the brain.

◁The heart pumps blood through your arteries to tiny blood vessels in every part of the body. It beats about 70 times a minute and never has a rest.

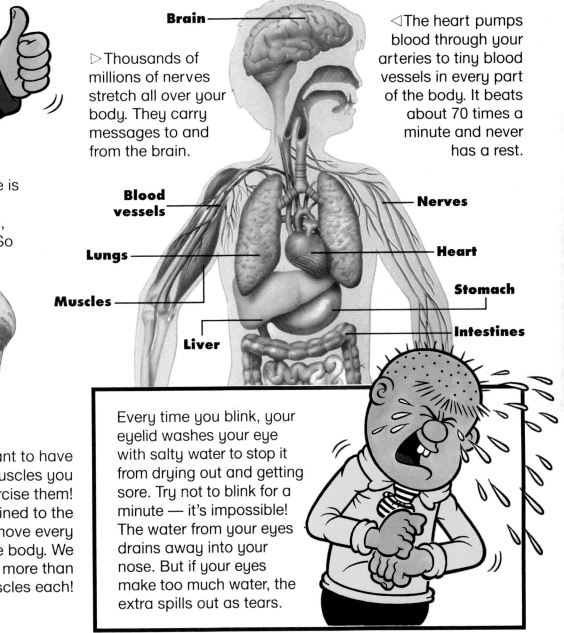

Brain
Blood vessels
Lungs
Muscles
Liver
Nerves
Heart
Stomach
Intestines

◁If you want to have bigger muscles you must exercise them! Muscles joined to the bones move every part of the body. We all have more than 650 muscles each!

Every time you blink, your eyelid washes your eye with salty water to stop it from drying out and getting sore. Try not to blink for a minute — it's impossible! The water from your eyes drains away into your nose. But if your eyes make too much water, the extra spills out as tears.

SPORTING SPECTACULARS

Sport is fun and it helps us to stay healthy. Everyone needs regular exercise to keep them fit. Professional athletes push their bodies to the limit. They train hard to run faster, jump further and do better than anyone has done before. Some sports are team games such as hockey, football or netball. Others like motor racing use complex and expensive equipment. Dennis is putting his athletic skill to good use, but most people play games just because they enjoy them. Others prefer to watch the excitement from the sidelines or on television.

Menacing Olympics!

▽ The world's most famous sporting event is the Olympic Games. Athletes from over 160 countries take part.

◁ The Tour de France is the toughest cycle race in the world. Cyclists pedal 4,000 km in just three weeks!

▷ Bungee jumping is a daring sport where competitors leap from great heights with thick, elastic ropes attached to their ankles. Think of poor Teacher's face!

▷ Football is the most popular sport, but it has changed a lot over the years. In the Middle Ages, boys played it in the street with a ball made from a pig's bladder!

HUMAN BODY

72

ATHLETIC FACTS

More people play and watch football than any other sport.

On a hot day, tennis players on Wimbledon's centre court sweat 1.5 litres of liquid each!

The first athlete to run a mile in under 4 minutes was the English runner Roger Bannister in 1954.

America's Nolan Ryan is the world's fastest baseball pitcher. At 162 km/h his throws would overtake most cars on a motorway.

The world's largest stadium is the Stahov Stadium in Prague, capital of the Czech Republic. It can hold 240,000 people!

In 1935 the American athlete Jesse Owens broke 6 world records in less than an hour.

The highest cricket score in a test match was England's 903 runs against Australia in 1938.

▽ The fastest team game is ice hockey. Players weave furiously across the ice slamming the puck.

△ In 1922 a British company invented golf balls with parachutes. It slowed the balls down and allowed golfers to practise at home without breaking any windows!

▽ The quickest people in sport are skydivers. They freefall at 300 km/h before they open up their parachutes.

◁ In Georgia they play lacrosse on horseback! Players gallop down the field, hurling the ball from net to net and into the goal.

Fencing!

Javelin!

JAVELIN EVENT

Diving!

75

BILLY'S WORLD TOUR

Our planet is divided into seven vast continents and over 170 countries. Only Billy Whizz could take a trip around the world on foot! Some are tiny islands such as Nauru, while others are giant countries like China, Canada and the biggest of all, Russia. Billy will need a map to find out where he is, but he will easily be able to tell when he moves from one country to another. Most countries have their own language and their own money. People living in cold countries dress differently from those in hot countries and every country has its own way of cooking food.

CONTINENTAL FACTS

Australia is the continent with the least amount of land, and the greatest amount of sea. It includes the countries of Australia, New Zealand and thousands of Pacific islands!

Asia, the biggest continent, is 4 times the size of Europe.

No one owns the frozen continent of Antarctica and no one lives there permanently.

To measure time around the world, the Earth is divided into 24 time zones. In each zone, time differs by 1 hour from the next. If you go east of the Greenwich Meridian it is later, but if you go west it is earlier!

One fifth of all the world's people live in China and about 48,000 new babies are born there every day!

In different parts of the world you might find almost anything on your plate — from insects and snails to snakes, guinea pigs or even sheep's eyes!

▷The Beano gang have learnt some new ways of saying 'good morning'. Which ones do you recognize? Around 5,000 languages and dialects are spoken world-wide. More people speak Chinese than any other language, although English is the most widely understood.

▽The Equator is an imaginary line drawn around the middle of the Earth. Lines of latitude measure distances north and south of the Equator. Lines of longitude measure distances east and west from the Greenwich Meridian. The Equator divides the Earth into Northern and Southern Hemispheres while the Greenwich Meridian divides it into Eastern and Western Hemispheres.

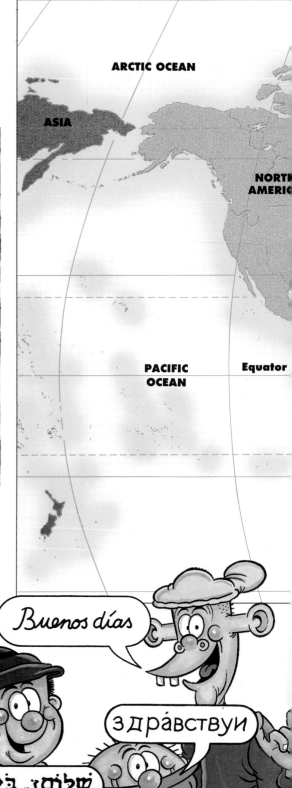

GOOD MORNING

jamm nga fënaan

Buenos días

здрáвствуи

שָׁלוֹם, בֹּקֶר טוֹב

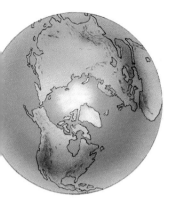

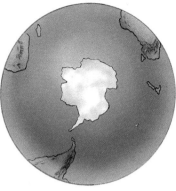
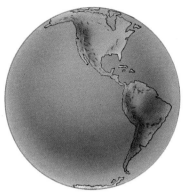

Northern Hemisphere   **Eastern Hemisphere**   **Southern Hemisphere**   **Western Hemisphere**

ARCTIC OCEAN

EUROPE

ASIA

ATLANTIC
OCEAN

PACIFIC
OCEAN

AFRICA

SOUTH
AMERICA

INDIAN OCEAN

Greenwich Meridian

AUSTRALIA

ANTARCTICA

WHIZZ AROUND EUROPE

Though Europe covers only seven per cent of the world's land, it is home to more people than North and South America combined. Europe has a great history and many of its cities are very old. Castles, cathedrals and palaces built hundreds of years ago are still standing today. Most Europeans live in cities and towns, but the continent has many natural beauties. The sights include Scottish lochs and Highlands, sunny Mediterranean seashores, Norwegian fiords and the towering snow-clad Alps. Even Billy would take months to explore them all!

△ The whole of Europe is in the Northern Hemisphere. Most of the continent has mild weather, but the countries in the south are much warmer than those in the north of Europe.

I'm going to long jump over the Channel!

Made it! I'm in France!

▽ At a Greek or Turkish wedding, the guests pin their wedding presents to the happy couple's clothes. The gifts are bank notes. Sometimes the bride and groom are covered from head to foot!

◁ The Russian statue *Motherland* is the biggest in the world. Standing 82 m high, she could hold an elephant in her outstretched hand!

▽ In Scotland each family, or clan, has a tartan with its own pattern and colour. Men wear tartan kilts to dance the Highland fling.

▽ These Portuguese fishermen have painted 'magic' fish-like eyes on their boats. They believe that the eyes will watch over them at sea and bring them safely home to harbour.

EUROPEAN FACTS

Europe's longest river, the Volga, and highest mountain, the Elbrus, are both in Russia.

One of the best known sites in Poland is the ancient salt mine in Wieliczka, near Cracow. It contains an old 17th century chapel carved entirely out of green salt!

Once a year in Pamplona in Spain a herd of fierce bulls is allowed to run through the streets, chasing anyone who dares to run before it.

The main streets of the Italian city of Venice are mostly canals. If you need a taxi, you can hire a motor boat or a water bus!

▽ The Tower of Pisa leans so far to one side it looks as if it might fall over. As the tower was built, the ground beneath it began to sink. But, so far, Italy's Leaning Tower of Pisa has stood for over 700 years!

◁ Once every year in November, the old city of Bern in Switzerland is turned into a huge onion market — over 100 tonnes of onions are put on sale! The Onion Festival also includes confetti battles, parades and fancy dress.

▷ Over 40,000 of these strange rocks make up the Giant's Causeway in Northern Ireland. Legend says that Finn MacCool (or Fingal) built it so that giants could cross from Ireland to Scotland without getting their feet wet!

Oops! I forgot they whizz on the other side of the road in France.

AN AMERICAN ADVENTURE

North and South America are two continents joined by a thin bridge of land. A towering range of mountains runs right down the west coast, from Alaska to the tip of South America. It is called the Rockies in the north and the Andes in the south. The Americas are so huge that Billy will travel through an amazing variety of climates and landscapes. Its peoples are varied too. Many of them emigrated there from Asia, Africa or Europe, although Native Americans have lived in the Americas for more than 20,000 years!

△ The Americas begin in the Arctic and almost stretch to the the Antarctic. They include also the Caribbean islands.

◁ These cheerful skeletons have been made to celebrate Mexico's Day of the Dead, a day when people remember dead loved ones.

▽ For special ceremonies, the Navajo people use coloured grains of sand to make beautiful pictures. They are said to be able to cure sick people who sit in the middle of them.

AROUND THE GLOBE

AMERICAN FACTS

In South America cowboys are called *gauchos*. They still round up cattle on horseback, but in the US, cowboys more often use a pick-up truck.

Some of Canada's wheatfields are bigger than small European countries!

The world's biggest waterfall is Angel Falls in Venezuela, South America. Here the water drops 979 m — over twice the height of the Sears Tower.

Mexico City is the largest city in the world. Over 20 million people live there, which is more than the entire population of Australia.

The Inuits, who live in the frozen wastes of northern Canada, have 20 different words for snow.

▷ Each year, during the famous and spectacular carnival of Rio de Janeiro in Brazil, thousands of people parade through the streets in glittering costumes.

▽Don't imitate King Kong and try to climb New York's Empire State Building. It is a dizzy 381 m tall! At 411 m the World Trade Centre, also in New York, is even taller. But the world's highest skyscraper is in Chicago. The Sears Tower looms 443 m above the street below.

▷In Bolivia and Peru, women wear round bowler hats as part of their national dress. These women live in the high mountains of the Andes and are paddling their reed boats across Lake Titicaca, the highest navigable lake in the world.

△The gigantic faces of four American presidents are carved into the granite cliffs of Mount Rushmore in South Dakota, USA. Washington, Jefferson, Roosevelt and Lincoln gaze down from their lofty height.

Can you find Billy in New York?

ON A SAFARI TRAIL

It is hot almost everywhere in Africa. The scorching Sahara Desert, the biggest and hottest in the world, covers most of North Africa. Near the Equator in the centre of the continent are thick rainforests. More than a third of Africa is a high, grassy plain. If Billy goes there on safari, he will see the world's last great herds of wild animals. The continent is often known as the cradle of humankind because the first humans came from Africa about four million years ago. Today, there are hundreds of different peoples in Africa, each with its own culture, language, religion and way of life.

△ The Equator passes across the centre of Africa. This huge continent covers one fifth of the world's land.

◁ These Masai people from Kenya are dressed up for a special celebration. The three young warriors are going to take part in a ceremony that will make them junior elders, marking their entry into manhood.

△ The river Nile is the world's longest river. It flows from central Africa down into the Mediterranean Sea. Its water makes farming possible in an area of desert.

AROUND THE GLOBE

AFRICAN FACTS

Did you know that both the tallest and the shortest groups of people in the world live in Africa? The average height of the Pygmies of central Africa is just 1.32 m, while the Nilotes from east Africa can be at least 2.10 m tall!

Desert people use sand, not water, to clean their dirty plates and pans.

In 1985, a fossil skeleton was discovered in Kenya. It had belonged to a boy and was 1,600,000 years old!

Africa's Sahara Desert is the biggest in the world. At over 9,000,000 sq km, it is 16 times the size of France.

There are 53 countries in Africa, more than in any other continent.

▽ Diamonds are mined in southern Africa. The biggest ever found was the Cullinan diamond— it weighed nearly three-quarters of a kilogram!

WHIZZ

▽ Don't wear beach clothes in the desert! There may be a lot of sand, but the Sun will fry your skin and, when the wind rises, stinging sand and dust are blown all around you. This is why desert people wear long, loose clothes that completely cover their faces and bodies.

△ The Great Mosque at Djenne in Mali, is made entirely out of sundried mud bricks! It was built in 1907 and is the largest earth building in the world.

▽ Fish is such an important food in Africa, that many people hold special festivals to celebrate the fishing harvest. Every year men from Argungu in Nigeria crowd into the water. They use dried gourds as floats and fish for giant perch.

ENORMOUS ASIA

Asia is easily the largest continent on Earth — it is so wide that the Sun rises almost 11 hours earlier in the east of the continent than it does in the west! Over half of all the world's people live there and yet most of Asia is barren, empty land. Desert covers much of the Middle East and China, and Siberia is a vast, freezing wilderness. Most people live in the south or east of Asia, but Billy might be surprised by their contrasting lifestyles. Huge cities in Japan, China and India are packed with people, while millions more live in villages and farm the land, following ancient ways of life.

△ Asia is bigger than Europe and Africa put together. This enormous continent stretches from the Arctic to the Equator and almost halfway around the world.

AROUND THE GLOBE

Phew! This is a big hill!

Argh! He's abominable!

▷ Let's hope Billy arrives in Kandy, Sri Lanka, on the night of the full moon in July! Then he will see this glittering parade of elephants, decorated with electric lights and beautiful cloths. These dancers and drummers are celebrating the festival of Esala Perahera.

△ The beautiful Taj Mahal in India is one of the world's most famous buildings. It was built over 300 years ago as a tomb for the wife of the emperor Shah Jahan. He employed 20,000 men to create the tomb, but it still took 20 years to build.

▷ This Japanese woman is dressed in a kimono for a special ancient tea ceremony called *chanoya*. The tea is made and sipped so slowly, that it can be hours before the drinking actually finishes!

ASIAN FACTS

The 100 highest mountains in the world are in Asia and 96 of those are in the Himalayas, between India and China. Mount Everest is the highest mountain of all.

You may be served cooked snake to eat in China and raw fish in Japan!

All the world's major religions — Hinduism, Judaism, Christianity, Islam and Buddhism — began in Asia.

More films are made in Bombay, India, than in Hollywood, USA.

Japanese people do not shake hands when they meet, they bow instead.

Lake Baikal in Russia is the deepest lake in the world. It is deep enough to drown Great Britain in at least 100 m of water.

Tokyo's trains are so crowded, that the city railway employs staff called 'crushers' to tightly pack people into the carriages!

▷In Saudi Arabia, huge crowds gather at desert racetracks to watch camel racing. These ungainly animals can gallop at over 20 km/h!

◁It takes lots of practice to dance as elegantly as this Indian dancer. She is wearing a sari made from a single piece of cloth wrapped around her body. It has no buttons, zips or even stitches.

◁The Great Wall of China was built over 2,000 years ago to keep out invading armies. But its wide, flat top also made it a very useful road. The Great Wall was built by hand and yet it stretches 6,400 km — making it the longest wall in the world!

▽Are giant pandas raccoons or bears? Even scientists aren't sure, but they do know that only a few now survive in the wild. This one is enjoying a stick of bamboo, but as farmers in China cut down the bamboo forests, there is now little left for pandas to eat.

DASHING DOWN UNDER

Australia is the only country that is also a continent. Its neighbours in the Pacific Ocean include Papua New Guinea, Tasmania, New Zealand and over 25,000 Pacific islands. Many of the islands are famous for their shimmering white beaches and swaying palm trees, but others have thick jungles and tall mountain peaks. Australia is known for its hot, dry climate. There's plenty of room for Billy to get some exercise here — the outback is so vast that children take their lessons by radio and doctors visit their patients by plane! New Zealand is much smaller, and it is made up of two islands, not one.

△ The continent of Australia is the smallest in the world. Many of the thousands of nearby Pacific islands are too tiny to show up on this map.

△ This Tahitian boy is holding up a net with a black pearl oyster inside. Local divers collect young oysters from the South Pacific Ocean and then cultivate them on floating farms.

▷ In Australia, there are more sheep than people! At the last count, there were 147 million sheep, which is over eight times the population of Australia. Some sheep farms are so large that farmers use planes to get around them!

BAA BAA BAA

◁ In Papua New Guinea, mud men dress up like this to represent bad spirits at a feast called a *singsing*. The island people believe that spirits of the dead can either punish them or help them. These strange masks were also once worn by warriors to scare away enemies.

AUSTRALIAN FACTS

Australia's Uluru (Ayers Rock) is an enormous 335 m high boulder. Its cave paintings were created thousands of years ago!

Papua New Guinea has over 700 different languages.

In New Zealand, it is a Maori custom to welcome guests by glaring and sticking your tongue out at them.

Red kangaroos are pests in Australia. They eat crops and cause accidents on roads.

In addition to its 2 main islands, Fiji is made up of about 800 small islands!

Lake Eyre is Australia's largest lake, but it is usually dry and covered in a hard salty crust that is up to 4 m thick.

I'm in a boomerang throwing competition!

Oops! That's going halfway round the world!

WHOOSH!

ZOOM! I'd better catch it!

▽ The Great Barrier Reef off the coast of Australia, is the largest structure ever created by a living thing. The coral is made of the skeletons of countless tiny sea animals.

▷ No one knows who carved this statue on Easter Island. There are 600 like this one — some are 20 m high! They were carved over 1,000 years ago.

▽ Sydney Opera House is one of the most unusual buildings in the world. It overlooks Sydney harbour and its roof was designed to look like sails billowing in the wind. The 'sails', however, are made from concrete covered with tiles.

△ A didgeridoo is an Aboriginal musical instrument which produces a deep, droning sound. Traditionally, it is made from a hollowed-out tree trunk — the centre has usually been eaten away by termites. Aborigines were the first people to settle in Australia. They have lived there for 40,000 years!

Back in Beanotown —

What kept you, boomerang?

BEANOTOWN MUSEUM

87

MORE AMAZING FACTS AND RECORDS

 JOURNEY INTO SPACE

The Moon is 100 times closer to Earth than any other planet in the Solar System.

Mercury and Venus are the hottest planets. Temperatures during the daytime soar above 450 °C.

Neptune and Pluto are the coldest planets in the Solar System because they orbit the furthest away from the heat of the Sun. Temperatures plunge below -200 °C!

The Milky Way spins like a mighty Catherine Wheel, but it takes 230 million years to complete 1 rotation. A black hole could lie at its centre.

The brightest comet to be seen regularly is Halley's comet. It passes the Sun every 76.1 years.

Most stars range from just a million to 10 billion years old, but the oldest known star could be 15 billion years of age!

 PLANET EARTH

The highest point in the world is Mount Everest in the Himalayas, Asia — its summit is 8,848 m above sea level.

Every year there are about 1,000 earthquakes worldwide that are strong enough to damage the Earth's surface.

At 6,670 km, the river Nile in Africa is the world's longest river. If all its bends were straightened out, it would flow from the Equator right up to northern Scotland!

The world's longest mountain range is the Andes of South America. It is also home for the world's highest active volcano — the 6,885 m high *Ojos de Salado*.

The lowest point on land is the shore of the Dead Sea in Asia. It lies 399 m below sea level.

The most enormous area of water on Earth is the colossal Pacific Ocean which spreads over 165 million sq km.

 LIVING WORLD

Protozoa are the smallest animals. Each has only one cell and is 0.002 mm long — a line of 500 would measure just 1 mm.

The world's most enormous fish is the whale shark. This harmless creature can weigh 15 tonnes!

The deadliest spider is probably the black widow of the Americas. Its poison is 15 times more powerful than the bite of a rattlesnake.

On a level flight, no bird on Earth can beat the spine-tailed swift. It is able to fly at a top speed of 170 km/h.

Cheetahs are the fastest animals on land. A cheetah can race at 112 km/h. It can sprint 100 m in less than 4 seconds.

The oldest living things are plants. The first plants were algae that appeared more than 3,000 million years ago. Flowering plants are modern — they first grew 150 million years ago!

 BACK IN TIME

65 million years ago, the dinosaurs died out, but no one knows why they became extinct.

10,000 years ago, people made an extraordinary discovery — farming. Instead of hunting they bred animals and planted crops. The first cities began to be built.

2,000 years ago, much of Europe, North Africa and the Middle East were ruled by the Roman Empire.

1,000 years ago, Vikings were still running riot in parts of northern Europe and Greenland.

500 years ago, adventurers were mapping the world.

200 years ago, the French were revolting against aristocrats and settlers in the USA had declared themselves independent.

50 years ago, World War II had just come to an end.

DISCOVER SCIENCE

The parts of an atom are unimaginably tiny. An atom's nucleus is 10,000 times smaller than the atom itself.

The energy provided by fossil fuels is in limited supply — geologists think there is only enough oil for about 30 years, enough gas for 55 years and enough coal for 200 years.

The Earth itself is a giant magnet, with its own north and south pole at either end.

Sound travels at 340 m a second, but planes can break this 'sound barrier'. The first supersonic flight was made in 1947 by Captain Charles Yeager in California, USA.

Light is split into just 7 colours, but they can be mixed to form over 10 million different shades visible to the human eye.

Gold is the stretchiest chemical element. Just a gram of gold can be drawn into a thread reaching over 2 km in length.

ON THE MOVE

The world's fastest car was propelled by a rocket. It reached a staggering 1,000 km/h.

The longest train journey you can make without changing trains is the 9,500 km from Moscow in Russia across to Nakhodka on the other side of the country. It takes 8 days.

The biggest hovercraft is the British SR-N4. Weighing over 305 tonnes, this giant can carry 400 passengers.

The X-15 from the USA is the world's fastest aeroplane. With an incredible top speed of 7,297 km/h, the plane has a rocket engine and has to be launched into the air.

Airships are more than 3 times as long as jumbo jets, even though the largest only carry 75 passengers.

The greatest car users live in the USA. On average, there is 1 car for every 2 people living there.

HUMAN BODY

You have about 14,000 million brain cells in your head, which act together to control your body. They are responsible for all of your thoughts, emotions and actions.

Adults have 3.5 to 6 litres of blood. Just a few drops contain about 7,500 white cells and 5,000 million red cells.

Your teeth are covered with enamel, the toughest substance in the human body.

About 9 m of intestines are rolled up inside every person.

The human ear has the ability to pick out more than 1,500 different musical tones.

Your skin is only about 2 mm thick over most of your body. The soles of your feet, however, are 3 mm thick.

The fastest human sprinter can run at just over 40 km/h.

AROUND THE GLOBE

Today the Earth is home to more than 5,000 million people. The daily increase in the world's population is about 256,000 — an average of 178 births per minute.

The Equator — the imaginary line around the middle of the Earth — is 40,091 km long.

The oldest town in the world is Jericho, southwest Asia. People have lived there for over 9,000 years.

Only 30 per cent of the world is land — the rest is ocean.

The most populated city in the world is Tokyo in Japan. By the year 2000, it should have 29,000,000 inhabitants.

Due to the world's time zones, when New Yorkers are eating breakfast at 8 am, Londoners are having lunch at 1 pm, Indonesians are eating dinner at 8 pm and New Zealanders are fast asleep at 1 am!

Entries in **bold** type refer to key topics. Page numbers in *italic* type refer to illustrations.

The publishers would like to thank the following artists
for contributing to this book:

J Adams; M Appleton; C Austin; J Baker; S Barclay;
B Corley; J Corville; J Cowne; R Draper; M Fisher;
E Flenny; E Fleury; R Flooks; C Forsey; O Frey; T Gabbey;
Garden Studios; P Goodfellow; J Gower; R Grinaway;
N Harris; I Jackson; K Johnstone; P Kelly; P Kestervan;
E Krähenbühl; T Lambert; C Lyon; K Maddison; A Marc;
J Marffy; A Male; A McBride; G Murry; S Noon; N Palin;
D Pattenden; S Quigley; E Rice; E Robinson; E Rowe;
N Shewring; R Shone; G Smith; C Spong; R Stewart;
M Taylor; I Thompson; A Winterbottom.

The publishers wish to thank the following for supplying
photographs for this book:

Page 15 The Planetarium; 16 Robert Harding; 18 ZEFA;
20 ZEFA; 23 Peter Rowlands; 50 Kobal; 51 ZEFA;
59 Streichan; 63 Bramaz; 81 ZEFA; 83 ZEFA.